Microeconomics Made Simple:

Basic Microeconomic Principles Explained in 100 Pages or Less

Why is there a light bulb on the cover?

In cartoons and comics, a light bulb is often used to signify a moment of clarity or sudden understanding—an "aha!" moment. The hope for the books in the *"...in 100 pages or less"* series is that they will help readers achieve clarity and understanding of topics that are often considered complex and confusing—hence the light bulb.

Microeconomics Made Simple:

Basic Microeconomic Principles Explained in 100 Pages or Less

Austin Frakt, PhD
Mike Piper, CPA

Disclaimer

The publisher and authors make no representation or warranty as to this book's adequacy or appropriateness for any purpose. Similarly, no representation or warranty is made as to the accuracy of the material in this book. Purchasing this book does not create any client relationship or other advisory, fiduciary, or professional services relationship with the publisher or with the authors. *You alone* bear the *sole* responsibility of assessing the merits and risks associated with any financial decisions you make.

Dedication

For you, the reader. We hope that this book provides you with more than enough utility to make it a worthwhile use of your resources.

Your Feedback Is Appreciated!

As the authors of this book, we're very interested to hear your thoughts. If you find the book helpful, please let us know. Alternatively, if you have any suggestions of ways to make the book better, we're eager to hear that, too.

Finally, if you're unhappy with your purchase for any reason, let us know, and we'll be happy to provide you with a refund of the current list price of the book (limited to one refund per title per household).

For any of these purposes, please email Mike at mike@simplesubjects.com.

Best regards,
Mike & Austin

Table of Contents

Microeconomics Made Simple

Introduction

Like the other books in the *"...in 100 Pages or Less"* series, this book is based on the assumptions that:

a) You want to gain a *basic* understanding of the book's topic (microeconomics), and
b) You want to achieve that basic level of understanding as quickly as possible.

For any students using this book in an academic setting: If your professor expects you to read a several-hundred-page textbook, please do not think that you can read this book instead and learn all of the same information. This book may serve as an introduction—a way to get a grip on the basics so that the textbook is easier to understand—but it's not meant to be a *replacement* for a comprehensive text.

For anybody interested in expanding upon the information contained in this book, additional resources can be found in Appendix A.

What Is Economics?

Each of us has limited resources. We have neither the time nor the money to do everything we might want to do. So we must choose: Out of all the possible options, on what will we spend our money and time?

Economics is the study of how people make these decisions. It asks how individuals, families, businesses, and governments decide how to allocate their limited (i.e., scarce) resources. In other words, economics is the study of how people deal with scarcity.

Economics is also concerned with incentives and their impact on behavior. Because we each have scarce resources (e.g., money), we're naturally motivated by the prospect of acquiring more resources. Economics looks at how this motivation to acquire more resources affects the decisions we make.

Macroeconomics vs. Microeconomics

*Macro*economics focuses primarily on decisions made by governments and trends in economic sectors in aggregate (e.g., housing, manufacturing, etc.), and the impacts of those decisions and trends on the overall national or global economy. For example, macroeconomics is often concerned with economic growth, unemployment, interest rates, and inflation. In contrast, *micro*economics—the topic of this book—focuses on the decisions made by individual people, families, and businesses.

Microeconomics includes examination of "markets"—places (whether physical or online) where goods[1] are exchanged between buyers and sellers (a.k.a. consumers and producers)—though it also includes other topics beyond the scope of this book (e.g., most of game theory). Fundamental to the study of markets are the questions: How much of a given good will consumers purchase? At what price(s)? And how are those quantities and prices affected by other factors?

For example, microeconomics could be used to study and describe the market for beer:

- How sensitive are consumers to changes in price? Do they buy significantly more if beer goes on sale? Will they cut back consumption dramatically if the price goes up?

- How do beer purchasers respond when the economy takes a nosedive? Do they drink more, because times are bad? Do they cut back, because they have less income? Or do they simply shift from craft beers to mass-market beers?

- How do brewers decide how much beer to produce and at what price to sell it? What

---

[1] For brevity's sake, throughout the book, we use the term "good" to refer to anything produced or sold, including tangible objects (e.g., cars, apples, pizza), intangible objects (e.g., downloadable software) and services (e.g., dental work, massages, landscaping).

would happen to the quantity of beer produced and its price if there were many more or many fewer producers of beer?

Economics: An Imperfect Model

Economics can be used to understand and predict the decisions people and other economic entities (e.g., businesses, governments) make. Though the insights of economics can be useful, each stems from a specific, approximate model of how the world works, and these models (like the models used in other fields) naturally deviate to some extent from how the real world actually works in detail.

Not all economics models make the same assumptions. In this book, we focus on basic models that assume economic entities are rational, have all relevant information for decision-making, and are able to fully understand and process that information. Assumptions like these obviously do not always hold in the real world. And other branches of economics not covered in this book—like behavioral economics—depart from them.

However, in order to best understand other areas of economics that make other assumptions, it helps to start with the basic models, however simplistic they may be.

Economics is also imperfect (or incomplete) in that it is not the only lens through which to view the world and judge the "correctness" of behaviors and outcomes. As we will explore, economics provides valuable tools to help individuals, businesses, governments, and other entities extract the greatest value their resources will allow. But economics does not generally deal directly with other important concepts like justice and equity, and it is sometimes at pains to explain cultural conventions (like the giving of birthday gifts instead of cash).

A strong understanding of economics includes facility with the models and concepts it offers, as well as an appreciation of their imperfections and limitations. We will highlight some of these limitations throughout this book and return to them in the conclusion.

What We'll Be Covering

This book is in two parts. In Part One, we will discuss several of the most basic concepts of economics, such as utility, supply, demand, market equilibrium, and some ways in which governments intervene in markets. At first, these concepts may seem unrelated as we introduce them. Rest assured, they'll all come into play later in the book. In Part Two, we'll focus on the degree of competition in different types of markets, as well as the outcome (in terms of price and quantity offered to consumers) of that competition. Market structures we will consider include: perfect competition, monopolies, oligopolies, and monopolistic competition.

Like many disciplines, economics has its own terminology. While we will of course define new terms the first time we use them in the text, you may still find the glossary at the end of the book (Appendix B) to be useful for quick reminders of definitions.

PART ONE

Basic Economic Concepts

CHAPTER ONE

Maximizing Utility

In economics, the word "utility" refers to a person's overall happiness or satisfaction. Economics assumes that each person's goal when allocating his or her resources is to make decisions to maximize his or her utility (i.e., achieve maximum happiness).

What about Charity?

Some people think that trying to maximize utility is the same thing as acting selfishly. In reality, however, utility *includes* the happiness, sense of fulfillment, or anticipated spiritual rewards that come from charitable acts. In other words, giving your time or money to a cause you believe in may in fact be the best way to maximize your utility. (And an economist would say that, given the opportunity to choose freely, you would only take such charitable actions if you believed that they *would* maximize your utility.)

Decreasing Marginal Utility

"Marginal utility" refers to how much additional utility is derived from consumption of one additional unit of a particular good. In theory, with each dollar in her budget, a rational person would buy the good that provides the highest marginal utility for that dollar (i.e., the most additional happiness per dollar).

The reason people do not spend all of their money on a single good is that consumption of most goods comes with decreasing marginal utility. "Decreasing marginal utility" is less complicated than it sounds. Think about how you feel when you take your first bite of your favorite pie: It makes you happy, offering you very high utility. What about after you've finished a slice and you're digging into your second? It doesn't make you quite as happy because you're fuller and the flavor is familiar. That is, the utility from the second slice is lower than the utility from the first. And it's lower still for a third slice. Each additional slice of pie provides less happiness (utility) than the previous slice. And, at some point, another slice of pie would actually bring *negative* utility (perhaps from a stomach ache). That is, you would actually be happier as a result of *not* eating that slice of pie.

Figure 1.1 illustrates what this would look like if we assume that you enjoy each of the first three slices (and it is the fourth that reduces your total utility). Notice that even though you enjoy the second slice, it doesn't add as much to your utility as the first slice did. The third adds even less. And the fourth slice actually brings negative marginal utility (i.e., it reduces your utility).

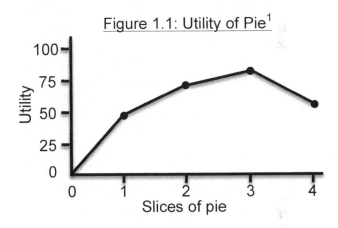

Figure 1.1: Utility of Pie[1]

---

[1] In Figure 1.1, the vertical axis is measured in something economists call "utils"—a hypothetical unit of utility.

Opportunity Cost

The "opportunity cost" of a choice is the value of the best alternative that you must forgo in order to make that choice.

Imagine that you are considering whether to go to a movie. Because your goal is to maximize your utility, and because staying at home and spending no money is always an option, you certainly won't go to a movie if the utility (i.e., happiness) you obtain from doing so isn't at least worth the ticket price and time spent. However, to make the best decision, it is not enough to think only of the dollar price of the ticket, how good the movie is, and how much time you'll spend watching it. You must also consider how much utility you would get from spending your resources— those dollars and that time you'd spend on the movie—in another way.

The "opportunity cost" of going to the movie is the forgone utility from the next most enjoyable activity you could have done (e.g., going out to eat, buying a video game, etc.). You will only choose to go to a movie if you think that the value of doing so (that is, the utility that it brings you) exceeds the opportunity cost of going to the movie (i.e., the utility that you would get from doing anything else with the time and money you would spend at that movie).

Chapter 1 Simple Summary

- In economics, it is assumed that each person's goal is to maximize his/her total "utility" (i.e., happiness).

- Most goods have decreasing marginal utility. That is, each additional unit consumed brings less additional happiness than the prior unit.

- To maximize utility, you must spend each dollar of your budget on the good that offers you the highest marginal utility for that dollar.

- Optimal decision making requires consideration of opportunity costs (i.e. the value of the forgone, best alternative option).

CHAPTER TWO

Evaluating Production Possibilities

In economics, "factors of production" are the inputs used to create finished goods (i.e., the actual products we buy). In other words, these are the scarce resources that we, as a society, must choose how to allocate. Ideally, we would do so in a way that maximizes our wellbeing. Traditionally, the factors of production are:

- Land (which includes land itself as well as other natural resources and phenomena—water, forests, fossil fuels, weather, etc.),
- Labor (the human work necessary to produce and deliver goods), and
- Capital (manmade goods used to produce other goods—factories, machinery, highways, electrical grid, etc.).

More recently, human capital—the knowledge and skills that make workers productive—has been considered a fourth factor of production.

How should a society allocate its factors of production? One desirable criterion is to use all resources to their fullest capacity or, to put it another way, to use the fewest possible resources for any given level of output (e.g., if a set of kitchen cabinets only requires 100 nails, a carpenter shouldn't pound in more). "Productive efficiency" is the term used to describe a situation in which this is achieved.

Another desirable criterion is that the factors of production are all used to make the quantities and types of goods that society most highly values. For example, if a society values the arts more highly than sports, it should invest more resources in the former than in the latter. "Allocative efficiency" is the term used to describe a situation in which productive resources are being used in their most valuable way.

Production Possibilities Frontier

A "production possibilities frontier" conveys the various choices that an economic entity[1] could

---

[1] For brevity's sake, we simply use the word "entity" to refer to any economic actor. The entity could be a person, family, business, state, country, etc.

make when choosing what to produce, given the constraint imposed by its limited factors of production. When considering possible combinations of two goods, those combinations can be illustrated graphically. Of course, entities frequently produce more than two different goods, but the important, basic concepts can be illustrated by considering just two goods at a time.

EXAMPLE: The following (hypothetical) production possibilities frontier shows the various quantities of apples and oranges that the state of Washington could produce in a year.

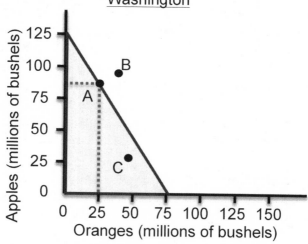

Figure 2.1: Production Possibilities Frontier: Washington

Points on the boundary between the shaded and unshaded region (e.g., Point A) use all resources available to Washington farmers (i.e., their factors of production) as efficiently as possible. Due to Washington's climate, oranges are difficult to grow there—requiring greenhouses, for example. Apples, on the other hand, grow more readily. Consequently, as the frontier shows, for Washington to increase its orange production by a little, it must decrease apple production by a lot. Specifically, for each increase of 25 million bushels in orange production, Washington must decrease apple production by just over 40 million bushels.

Points outside the shaded region (e.g., Point B) are impossible for Washington to reach with its own resources—this is why the line is known as the production possibilities *frontier*. Points within the shaded region (e.g., Point C) are not "productively efficient." That is, at such points, the state would not be using all of its available resources efficiently.

Naturally, Washington wants to produce apples and oranges in some combination along its production possibilities frontier. (It cannot produce beyond the frontier, and it would not be productively efficient to produce below the frontier.) *Which* specific point along the frontier it chooses is dictated by allocative efficiency—it's whatever combination of apples and oranges would bring the state's citizens the most utility (ignoring the possibility of importing or exporting fruit).

Now let's take a look at the apples/oranges production possibilities frontier for Florida:

Figure 2.2: Production Possibilities Frontier: Florida

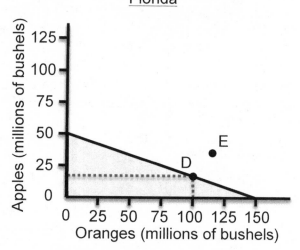

Due to differences in climate and other resources, Florida has a different set of possible, productively efficient apple-orange production combinations than Washington. Specifically, Florida has a relatively easier time growing oranges and a harder time growing apples. For each increase of 25 million bushels in apple production, the state must decrease orange production by about 75 million bushels.

If the residents of each state want some apples and some oranges, what should they do? One possibility is that each state could grow some of each fruit. For example, Washington could grow 25 million bushels of oranges and 83.3 million bushels of apples (Point A on Washington's production possibilities frontier), and Florida could grow 100 million bushels of oranges and 16.7 million bushels of apples (Point D on Florida's production possibilities frontier). Combined output across the two states would be 100 million bushels of apples and 125 million bushels of oranges. Let's call this the "no specialization" scenario (see the following table).

	No specialization	Specialize & trade
Washington	83.3 apples 25 oranges	90 apples 35 oranges
Florida	16.7 apples 100 oranges	35 apples 115 oranges
Total	100 apples 125 oranges	125 apples 150 oranges
Values are hypothetical and in millions of bushels.		

Another approach is for each state to specialize and trade. That is, Washington could commit entirely to apple production, growing a total of 125 million bushels of apples, and Florida could grow only oranges—150 million bushels of them, to be precise. Notice that this is a higher total output than they produced when each grew both kinds of fruit. They could then trade 35 million bushels of fruit on a one-for-one basis. This would give Washington 90 million bushels of apples and 35 million bushels of oranges (Point B, outside its production possibilities frontier). It would give Florida 35 million bushels of apples and 115 million bushels of oranges (Point E, outside its production possibilities frontier). By specializing and trading, each state is left with more apples and more oranges than they would have if they tried to produce both fruits on their own. Without trade, an entity cannot obtain (or consume) more than the quantities that lie on its production possibilities frontier.

This lesson is one of the most critical insights of economics. Specialization and trade makes everybody better off. In a world with few constraints on trade, we're better off with doctors, farmers, and homebuilders than we would be if everybody tried to handle their own medical needs, grow their own food, and make their own home.

Absolute Advantage and Comparative Advantage

If it takes you fewer units of input (e.g., hours of labor, acres of land, etc.) to make a given product than it takes your neighbor Bob to make that same product, you are said to have an "absolute advantage" over Bob in the production of that product. The previous example of apple and orange production in Washington and Florida can be used to illustrate absolute advantage. If we assume that the two states have the same level of inputs at their disposal for apple and orange production, Washington has an absolute advantage over Florida in apple production because it requires fewer inputs per apple than Florida. (That is, it can produce more apples with the same input.) Conversely, Florida has an absolute advantage over Washington in the production of oranges.

It's tempting to conclude that it is Washington's absolute advantage in apples and Florida's absolute advantage in oranges that explains why the states gain from trade. Interestingly, however, an entity can specialize and gain from trade even if it does *not* have an absolute advantage in anything. To be more specific, it makes sense to specialize in something if you have a "comparative advantage" in it—that is, your *opportunity cost* for producing that thing is lower than that of other potential producers.

EXAMPLE: Suppose the arrival of a new insect to Florida causes orange production to require more inputs than illustrated in the previous example (e.g., more insecticide and special handling). Given its available resources, instead of being able to produce 150 million bushels of oranges, now the state can only produce 62.5 million bushels, which is 12.5 million bushels fewer than Washington state could produce if it specialized in oranges.

Figure 2.3: New Production Possibilities Frontier: Florida

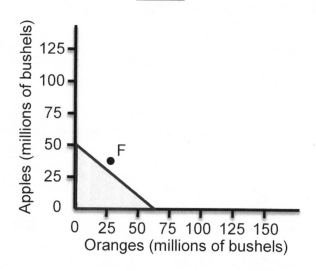

Now Washington has an absolute advantage over Florida in both apple and orange production. Still, both states can gain by specializing and trading.

Suppose Washington again specialized in apples, producing 125 million bushels of them, and Florida in oranges, now producing just 62.5 million bushels of them. Then, if the states again traded 35 million bushels of fruit on a one-for-one basis, Washington would end up, again, with 90 million bushels of apples and 35 million bushels of oranges (Point B in Figure 2.1), and Florida would end up with 35 million bushels of apples and 27.5 million bushels of oranges (Point F in Figure 2.3). Because both Points B and F are outside the states' respective production possibilities frontiers, both states are made better off by specializing and trading.

Due to *comparative* advantage, gains from trade are possible even for an entity that does not have an absolute advantage in anything (as is the case with Florida, after the insect infestation). For each unit of orange production, Florida, after the insect infestation, gives up the opportunity to produce 0.8 units of apples. (That is, Florida's opportunity cost for producing one orange is 0.8 apples.) In contrast, because Washington is so darned good at making apples, for each unit of orange production, it must give up the opportunity to produce 1.66 apples. (That is, Washington's opportunity cost for producing one orange is 1.66 apples.) Because Florida has a lower *opportunity cost* for orange production, it has a comparative advantage over Washington in the production of oranges. And because of this comparative advantage, Florida still gains from specializing and trading.

Chapter 2 Simple Summary

- Factors of production (land, labor, capital, and human capital) are limited resources that a society must choose how to allocate.

- A production possibilities frontier shows all combinations of two goods that an entity can produce with its factors of production.

- Through specialization and trade, an entity can consume more than its production possibilities frontier implies in isolation.

- A producer has an absolute advantage in producing a good if it can produce it with fewer inputs than other producers require.

- A producer has a comparative advantage in producing a good if it can produce it at a lower *opportunity cost* than other producers.

- Gains from trade are possible due to comparative, not absolute, advantages.

CHAPTER THREE

Demand

The "demand" for a good is simply how much of that good consumers would buy at various prices. Demand is often illustrated using a graph known as a "demand curve." (It's referred to as a curve even when the graph is a straight line.)

EXAMPLE: The following is Bob's monthly demand curve for frozen pizza. Note that demand curves can be read in either direction. That is, in addition to showing how many frozen pizzas Bob would buy per month at a given price, this demand curve also shows how much Bob would be willing to pay per pizza for a given number of pizzas. For example, Bob would be willing to pay $4 per pizza for 4 pizzas per month.

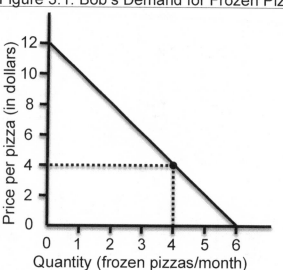

Figure 3.1: Bob's Demand for Frozen Pizza

In addition to graphing an individual's demand curve for a good, we can graph the market demand curve for a good, which would show how much of that good would be purchased, collectively, by everyone at each unit price. The market demand for a good is simply the aggregate (or sum) of every individual consumer's demand for that good.

Elasticity of Demand

Demand curves naturally tend to be downward sloping, indicating that the higher the price of the good in question, the less of it people will buy.

The steepness of a demand curve illustrates how sensitive consumers are to changes in the price of the good. If a demand curve is relatively flat, consumers are highly price sensitive, meaning that when the price goes up (or down) even slightly, they dramatically decrease (or increase) the quantity they purchase. Goods of this nature are said to have very "elastic demand."[1] If a good has a horizontal demand curve, its demand is said to be "perfectly elastic."

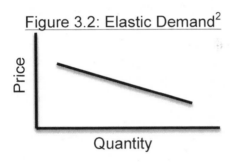

Figure 3.2: Elastic Demand[2]

---

[1] Though related, "elasticity" and "slope" are different, as elasticity is the *percentage* change in quantity demanded, divided by the *percentage* change in price.

[2] In economics, charts are often drawn without extending the curves all the way to the axes. This is done so that we don't have to illustrate the bizarre effects that occur near the axes (e.g., the fact that at a price of zero, quantity demanded is basically infinite).

Conversely, some goods have very steep demand curves, indicating that consumers are *not* very sensitive to changes in the price of the good. That is, even when the price goes up (or down) significantly, they only slightly decrease (or increase) the quantity they purchase. Goods of this nature are said to have "inelastic demand." If a good's demand curve is vertical, its demand is said to be "perfectly inelastic."

Figure 3.3: Inelastic Demand

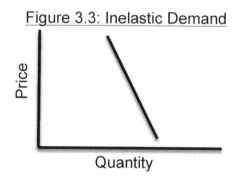

There are multiple factors that affect the elasticity of demand for a good, such as:

- Availability of substitutes,
- Whether the good is a necessity or a luxury,
- Whether the good is a small or large part of buyers' overall budgets, and
- Time.

When there are many acceptable substitutes for a good, demand for that good tends to be highly elastic. For example, demand for any particular brand of toothpaste is probably quite elastic. If the price goes up significantly, most consumers would be perfectly happy to switch to a different brand. Conversely, the demand for toothpaste *overall* is probably much less elastic. If the price for all brands of toothpaste increased, consumers would probably not cut back dramatically on their toothpaste consumption, because there's little in the way of acceptable substitutes for toothpaste.

In economics, goods are often classified as either luxury goods or necessities. All else being equal, a luxury good (e.g., jewelry) would have a higher elasticity of demand than a necessity (e.g., a life-saving drug).

The more of one's budget a good requires (due to high price and/or large quantity used), the more sensitive one would be to changes in its price (i.e., the more elastic demand would be). For example, if the price of new cars were to increase by 30%, many consumers who were planning to purchase a car this year would choose to delay their purchase. In contrast, a 30% increase in the price of potatoes would probably have a much smaller effect on people's purchasing decisions—many potato buyers probably wouldn't even notice the change in price.

Finally, the elasticity of demand for a good is generally higher over a long period of time than over a short period. Shortly after the price of a good increases, for example, consumers may simply continue their past buying habits because that's the easiest thing to do. In contrast, after some time, consumers begin to view the new, higher price as permanent, and they put more effort into looking for substitutes.

"Change in Demand" as Opposed to "Change in Quantity Demanded"

When the price of a good changes, the resulting change in how much of it people want to buy is referred to as a "change in the quantity demanded." Such changes are indicated by a movement *along* the good's demand curve.

In contrast, a "change in demand" is a shift *of* the demand curve, caused by changes in factors other than the good's price. A decrease in demand is a shift of the demand curve to the left, meaning that, at any given price, consumers would demand less of the good than they demanded at that price previously. Conversely, an increase in demand is a shift of the demand curve to the right, meaning that at any given price, consumers would demand more of the good than they would have demanded at that price in the past.

EXAMPLE: In Figure 3.4, the line D_1 is the market demand curve for frozen pizza. If the price of a pizza were to increase from $4 to $10, the result would be a decrease in the *quantity demanded*—a movement *along* the demand curve from Point A to Point B.

However, if pizza were discovered to cause a previously-unknown health problem, consumers would want less of it at every price. That is, there would be a *decrease in demand*, shown as a shift of the demand curve to the left (e.g., from D_1 to D_2).

Figure 3.4: Frozen Pizza: Change in Quantity Demanded vs. Change in Demand

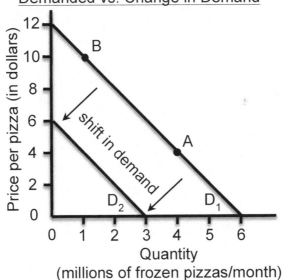

Several factors can cause a shift in demand:

- Changes in consumer preferences,
- Changes in consumer income levels,
- Changes in the prices of other goods,
- Changes in consumer expectations, and
- Changes in the number of consumers in the market.

Changes in consumer preferences affect the demand for a good in very intuitive ways. When a fashion-related item comes into style, demand for it goes up. When a new product makes an old product obsolete, demand for the old product falls (i.e., the old product's demand curve shifts to the left). When research is released showing that a particular food is good for your health, demand for that food increases (i.e., the demand curve for the food shifts to the right). You get the idea.

For most goods, when consumer income levels increase, demand for the good increases. Goods of this nature are said to be "normal goods." Some goods, however, are known as "inferior goods." For these goods, demand actually *decreases* when consumer income rises. Inferior goods tend to be at the low end of the cost and quality spectrums (e.g., Ramen noodles or Spam).

If Coke goes on sale, demand for Pepsi falls. Coke and Pepsi are known as "substitute goods."

They are similar enough to one another that one can readily serve as a substitute for the other. When the price of one decreases, demand for the substitute decreases. And when the price of one increases, demand for the substitute increases.

Conversely, "complementary goods" behave in the opposite manner to substitute goods. Hot dogs and hot dog buns are the classic example. They go together, or "complement" one another. When one goes on sale, demand for the other increases. And if the price of one were to increase, demand for the other would decrease.

Consumer expectations affect demand as well. If consumers expect the price of a good to go up in the near future, they stock up on it now (i.e., demand increases right now). Conversely, if consumers expect the price to go down in the near future, consumers choose to delay their purchases (i.e., current demand decreases).

Finally, demand for a good changes when the number of buyers in the market changes. For example, if enrollment goes up dramatically at a given university, demand for rental housing in the nearby area will increase.

Chapter 3 Simple Summary

- The demand curve for a product shows the quantity of that product that consumers would buy at various prices.

- When demand for a good is elastic, the quantity that consumers want to buy is more sensitive to price changes. When demand for a good is inelastic, the quantity purchased is less sensitive to price changes.

- A change in the quantity demanded is a movement *along* the demand curve due to a price change. A change in demand is a shift *of* the demand curve due to changes in factors other than the price of the good.

- Demand can change in response to changes in factors such as consumer preferences, income levels, expectations, number of buyers in the market, and prices of other goods.

- When the price of a good goes up, demand for its substitutes goes up and demand for its complements goes down.

CHAPTER FOUR

Supply

The "supply" for a good is how much of that good producers would produce at various prices. Like demand, supply is often illustrated via a graph—known as a "supply curve" in this case. One can draw a supply curve for an individual producer, just as one can draw a demand curve for an individual consumer. Similarly, one can aggregate across all producers of the same good (or very similar goods) to get a market supply curve.

EXAMPLE: The following hypothetical supply curve shows how many frozen pizzas Pauline's Pies would produce at various prices. As with demand curves, supply curves can be read in either direction. That is, in addition to showing how much suppliers would produce at a given price, supply curves show how much producers must be paid (per unit) to produce a given quantity. For example, this supply curve not only shows that Pauline would produce 1,000 frozen pizzas per month at $6 per pizza, it also shows that a price of $6 per pizza is the minimum that Pauline would need to be paid in order to produce 1,000 pizzas per month.

Figure 4.1: Pauline's Pies' Supply of Frozen Pizza[1]

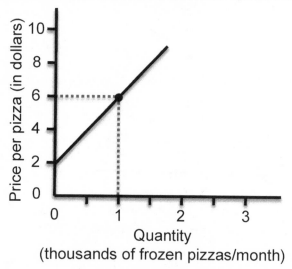

Quantity
(thousands of frozen pizzas/month)

---

[1] Notice that the axes in this chart are the same as for the demand charts from Chapter 3. These two axes (units of the good in question on the horizontal x-axis and dollars on the vertical y-axis) are very common in economics charts. We will be using them throughout the rest of the book, so it's worth taking the time to become familiar with them.

How Costs Affect Supply

Generally, to entice a firm to produce a given quantity of a good, you must pay the firm an amount sufficient to cover its costs of production.

EXAMPLE: Pauline's Pies can produce 1,000 frozen pizzas per month, at a cost of $6,000 (i.e., $6 per pizza). So, at an output level of 1,000 pizzas per month, what is the very lowest price that Pauline would be willing to accept? $6 per pizza.

If Pauline has her employees work overtime every day, the business can produce 1,500 pizzas per month. But, because Pauline pays her workers "time and a half" for overtime, her cost per pizza would rise to $8. In other words, in order to entice Pauline to produce 1,500 pizzas per month, consumers would have to pay her $8 per pizza.

As you can see, Pauline's supply curve for frozen pizzas is *upward* sloping. That is, the business requires a higher price per unit in order to produce a higher level of output.

The "marginal cost of production" for a good is the additional cost that must be incurred in order to produce one more unit of the good. The supply curves for most goods are upward sloping because most industries face "increasing marginal costs of production," meaning that each additional unit of production costs more than the unit before (as is the case with Pauline's production of pizzas).

Elasticity of Supply

"Elasticity of supply" refers to how sensitive producers are to changes in price. If a slight increase in price draws many new producers into the market (or persuades existing ones to increase production dramatically), supply for the good is said to be elastic. If a good has a horizontal supply curve, its supply is said to be "perfectly elastic."

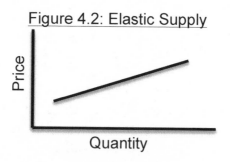

Figure 4.2: Elastic Supply

Conversely, if a change in price only results in a very slight change in the quantity that producers are willing to supply, the good is said to have inelastic supply. If a good has a vertical supply curve, its supply is said to be "perfectly inelastic."

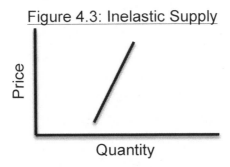

Figure 4.3: Inelastic Supply

The elasticity of supply for a good is determined by how easy it is for producers to change their level of output in response to changes in price. The easier and less costly it is for producers to change output, the more elastic supply would be.

For example, if production of a good requires an input that is only available in limited quantities (e.g., heart transplants, which require viable hearts), it would be difficult for producers to ramp up production to respond to a price increase. In other words, supply is inelastic.

Conversely, if the major input is unskilled labor or other easy-to-access commodities (e.g., in the production of printer paper), producers would have an easier time adjusting their levels of output based on changes in price. In other words, supply is very elastic.

Elasticity of supply (like that of demand) tends to be greater in the long run than in the short run because producers have an easier time adjusting output levels when given more time to do so (e.g., to build more factories, train more workers, etc.).

"Change in Supply" as Opposed to "Change in Quantity Supplied"

When the price of a good changes, the resulting change in how much of it producers want to produce is said to be a "change in the quantity supplied." Such changes are indicated by movements *along* the good's supply curve.

In contrast, a "change in supply" is a shift *of* the supply curve, caused by changes in factors other than the good's price. For example, an increase in supply would be shown as a shift of the supply curve to the right, indicating that at every price, suppliers would produce more of the good than they previously produced at that price. Said differently, producers would be willing to accept a lower price for any quantity.

EXAMPLE: Pauline's Pies reconfigures its kitchen, using a more efficient layout that allows for more pizzas to be produced per hour of labor. As a result of the change, Pauline's cost of production decreases. Now, at any given quantity, Pauline can accept a lower price than she would have accepted previously. Or, if you read the following Figure 4.4 in the other direction, Pauline's Pies will now produce more pizzas at any given price than the business would have produced previously. For example, at a price of $6, it would have produced 1,000 pizzas per month before (supply curve S_1), whereas now it will produce 1,750 pizzas per month (supply curve S_2).

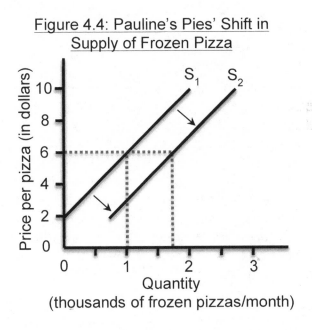

Figure 4.4: Pauline's Pies' Shift in Supply of Frozen Pizza

In contrast to the above example, a *decrease* in supply is shown as a movement of the supply curve to the *left*, meaning that at every price, suppliers are willing to produce *less* of the good than they were willing to produce at that price previously.[1]

Changes in supply can be caused by several factors, including:

- Changes in costs of production,
- Changes in opportunity costs,
- Changes in supplier expectations, and
- Changes in the number of suppliers.

As we saw with Pauline's Pies, a decrease in cost of production (e.g., due to new technology) results in an increase in the supply of that good. In contrast, an increase in the cost of production (e.g., an increase in the price of tomatoes, in the case of pizza production) results in a decrease in supply.

The supply of a good can also be affected by changes in opportunity costs. For example, if the profit margin for producing frozen ravioli were to increase, the supply of frozen pizzas would fall (i.e., the supply curve for frozen pizzas would shift

---

[1] Remember, because quantity is on the horizontal x-axis, increases and decreases in supply are easiest to think of as leftward or rightward movements of the supply curve. It's tempting to think that an increase in supply would be an upward movement of the supply curve, but that would actually be a *decrease* in supply, as it would mean that a higher price is required in order to get producers to produce any given quantity.

to the left) as producers moved resources from frozen pizza production to frozen ravioli production. That is, the opportunity cost for producing frozen pizzas increases when the profitability of producing frozen ravioli increases. As a result, the supply of frozen pizzas goes down.

If suppliers expect the price of their product to increase in the near future, they may choose to decrease supply, holding on to some of their inventory in the hope of selling it at tomorrow's higher price rather than sell it at today's price.

A change in supply can also be the result of a change in the number of suppliers. For example, if a pharmaceutical company's patent on a drug expires, new companies will enter the market for that drug (i.e., there would be an increase in the number of suppliers). This would cause an increase in the supply of the drug. That is, the supply curve would shift to the right, meaning that more of the drug would be produced (supplied) at any given price than would have been produced at that price previously. Or stated differently (because supply curves can be read in either direction), the minimum price necessary to get producers to supply a given amount of the drug would be lower than the price that would have been necessary before the influx of new suppliers.

Chapter 4 Simple Summary

- A good's supply curve shows the quantity producers would produce at various prices.

- A good's marginal cost of production is the additional cost that must be incurred to produce one additional unit of the good.

- Most supply curves are upward sloping because most goods have increasing marginal costs of production.

- When supply for a good is elastic, the amount producers will produce is more sensitive to price changes. When supply for a good is inelastic, the amount producers will make is less sensitive to prices changes.

- A movement *along* the supply curve due to a change in price is a change in the quantity supplied. A shift *of* the supply curve is a change in supply due to changes in factors other than the good's price.

- Supply can change in response to changes in any of several factors: costs of production, opportunity costs, supplier expectations, or the number of suppliers.

CHAPTER FIVE

Market Equilibrium

When you plot a good's market demand curve and market supply curve on the same graph, the point at which the curves meet is especially important. At this price (known as the "equilibrium price"), the quantity of the good that producers are willing to supply is equal to the quantity of the good that consumers are willing to buy. This quantity is known as the "equilibrium quantity." This point—the point at which quantity supplied and quantity demanded are equal—is referred to as the "equilibrium point."

Market equilibrium is a desirable outcome. It means that everybody who wants to buy the good at its current price is able to find somebody to sell it to them, and it means that everybody who wants to supply the good at its current price is able to find somebody to buy their product. This is also referred to as a "market clearing" outcome.

EXAMPLE: The following figure shows the market equilibrium for frozen pizza, the point at which the total quantity supplied of frozen pizza is equal to total quantity demanded for it.

Figure 5.1: Supply and Demand of Frozen Pizza

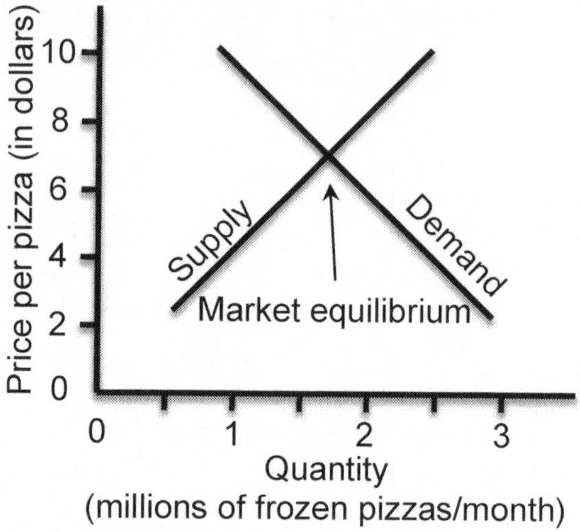

How Market Equilibrium Is Reached

In a market in which buyers and sellers are permitted to act without constraints (often called a "free market") their actions drive the price and quantity of a good toward market equilibrium.[1]

---

[1] In some markets, buyers and sellers *are* constrained, as we will discuss in the next chapter.

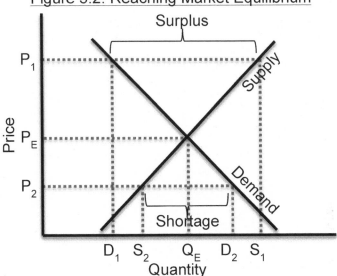

Figure 5.2: Reaching Market Equilibrium

Figure 5.2 shows supply and demand curves for a good that intersect at price P_E and quantity Q_E, the equilibrium price and quantity, respectively. Imagine that the price of the good is currently P_1, which is higher than P_E. At P_1, suppliers would produce quantity S_1 units, but consumers would only buy quantity D_1 units. In other words, there would be a surplus, as illustrated in Figure 5.2.

In the event of a surplus, what do suppliers naturally do? They have a sale (i.e., reduce prices) to get rid of excess inventory. And in the event of a surplus, what do consumers naturally do? They try to negotiate prices downward. Both of these actions continue until the price of the good has come down to the market equilibrium price (P_E)—at which point the surplus is gone because quantity supplied is equal to quantity demanded (Q_E).

Now let's imagine that the price of the good in Figure 5.2 is currently P_2, which is *lower* than the equilibrium price P_E. At P_2, consumers of the good would be willing to purchase quantity D_2 units. Suppliers, however, would only produce quantity S_2 units at P_2. In other words, there would be a shortage, as illustrated in Figure 5.2.

In the event of a shortage, what do consumers naturally do? They offer to pay more. And in the event of a shortage, what do suppliers naturally do? They raise prices to preserve inventory (and to earn higher profits). Both of these actions continue until the price of the good has been brought up to the market equilibrium price (P_E)—at which point the shortage is gone because quantity supplied is equal to quantity demanded (Q_E).

The Effect of Changes in Supply and Demand

When we graph a good's supply and demand together, not only can we determine the market equilibrium price and quantity, we can also determine how the equilibrium changes when supply or demand for the good changes.

EXAMPLE: Figure 5.3 shows the effect of an increase in demand. When the demand curve shifts to the right (from D_1 to D_2), it intersects the supply curve (S) at a different point. That is, the price of the good increases (from P_1 to P_2), as does the equilibrium quantity (from Q_1 to Q_2).

Figure 5.3: Market Equilibrium and Demand Shift

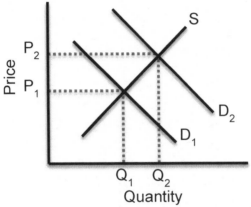

Conversely, when demand decreases, the demand curve shifts to the left (e.g., from D_2 to D_1 in the previous graph), and there is a decrease in the equilibrium price of the good (from P_2 to P_1) and in the equilibrium quantity (from Q_2 to Q_1).

EXAMPLE: When the supply for a good increases, as in Figure 5.4 (from S_1 to S_2), there is an increase in the equilibrium quantity (from Q_1 to Q_2), but a decrease in the equilibrium price (from P_1 to P_2).

Figure 5.4: Market Equilibrium and Supply Shift

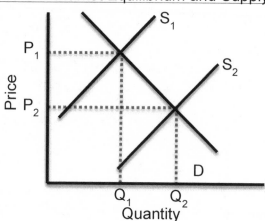

Conversely, when the supply for a good decreases (e.g., from S_2 to S_1 in the prior graph), there is a decrease in the equilibrium quantity (from Q_2 to Q_1), but an increase in the equilibrium price (from P_2 to P_1).

Rather than try to memorize the impact on price and quantity caused by increases and decreases in supply and demand, it's much easier to simply sketch a quick graph, then shift one of the lines (supply or demand, as applicable) in the necessary direction to see what happens.

Chapter 5 Simple Summary

- At the market equilibrium point for a good, quantity supplied and quantity demanded are equal.

- Unconstrained buyers and sellers acting in their best interests drive a market to equilibrium.

- A shift in demand or supply affects both the equilibrium price and quantity of a good. The easiest way to determine the effect is to sketch a graph with the original and shifted curves.

CHAPTER SIX

Government Intervention

As we've just seen, in a free market, buyers and sellers acting in their own interests have the (unintended) effect of driving prices and quantities to their equilibrium levels. For various reasons, however, this does not always occur. For instance, a government choosing to intervene in a market (e.g., by taxing or subsidizing the good) is one, but not the only, way a market can fail to reach free-market equilibrium.

Price Floors and Price Ceilings

In some cases, the government imposes a mini-mum price on a good—a "price floor." In such a case, if the price floor is above the equilibrium price, there would be a surplus of the good. That is, supply and demand for the good would look like the surplus situation illustrated in Figure 5.2 of the previous chapter, but market forces would not be able to move the price and quantity toward equilibrium. A surplus is not desirable because it wastes resources, as more is produced than gets purchased—though, as discussed below, society sometimes decides that a price floor is worthwhile anyway due to other factors.

In other cases, the government imposes a maximum price on a good—a "price ceiling." If the price ceiling is below the equilibrium price, there would be a shortage of the good. That is, the supply and demand for the good would look like the shortage situation illustrated in the previous chapter (again, Figure 5.2), but market forces would not be able to move the price and quantity toward equilibrium. A shortage is not desirable because people cannot obtain the goods they want to purchase—though again, society sometimes decides that a price ceiling is worthwhile due to other factors.

Despite the generally undesirable nature of surpluses and shortages, our society sometimes chooses to impose price floors and ceilings. (Whether the benefits outweigh the drawbacks is often a matter of debate, even among economists.) For example, the minimum wage is a price floor for labor, and polls indicate that it is supported by a majority of Americans. And, at various points in time, certain communities have implemented rent control programs (i.e., price ceilings on rent).

Taxes and Subsidies

Many goods are taxed or subsidized by the government. Just like price ceilings and floors, taxes and subsidies move the transaction price and quantity supplied and demanded away from the free-market equilibrium. And, just like price ceilings and floors, that can be illustrated in a supply-demand graph.

Let's consider taxes first. In the absence of a tax on a good, the price the consumer pays is equal to the revenue the seller receives. However, when a tax—like a sales tax—is imposed, the total price the consumer pays is *greater* than the revenue the seller ultimately receives, after paying the tax to the government. More specifically, the revenue received by the supplier is equal to the total price paid by the consumer, minus the applicable tax.

EXAMPLE: In Figure 6.1, prior to the implementation of a tax, the market is in equilibrium at P_E and Q_E. But what would happen if the government decided to implement a tax on the sale of the good? What would be the effect on the price customers would pay, the revenue sellers would receive, and the quantity bought and sold?

In the presence of a tax, we know that the revenue received by the sellers must be equal to the total price paid by consumers, minus the amount of the tax. So, to find the new post-tax equilibrium, we must find the quantity at which consumers' willingness to pay (as shown by the demand curve) is higher than the minimum amount suppliers would be willing to accept (as shown by the supply curve) by an amount equal to the tax. For example, if the tax were \$5 per unit, we would find the quantity at which the demand curve is \$5 higher than the supply curve. In Figure 6.1, Q_T designates the quantity of the good that would be transacted in the presence of the tax.

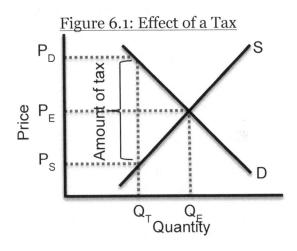

Figure 6.1: Effect of a Tax

As you can see from Figure 6.1, relative to the free-market (no tax) equilibrium, the net effect of a tax

is to raise the purchase price (from P_E to P_D) and reduce the seller's revenue (from P_E to P_S). The difference between P_D and P_S is the value of the tax. Also, as shown, a tax reduces the quantity bought/sold (from Q_E to Q_T).

As shown in Figure 6.2, a per-unit subsidy—in which the government supplements seller revenue—has the opposite effect of a tax. This isn't especially surprising, given that a subsidy is just a tax in reverse. Relative to the free-market equilibrium, a subsidy raises the quantity transacted (to Q_S in Figure 6.2), reduces the price paid by the consumer (to P_D), and increases the revenue received by the supplier (to P_S). The subsidy is the difference between the supplier's revenue (P_S) and the purchase price (P_D).

Figure 6.2: Effect of a Subsidy

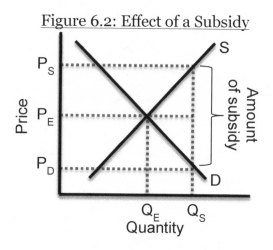

Interestingly, the tax-related chart from earlier in this chapter (Figure 6.1) would look the same whether the tax were imposed on the buyer or on the seller. That is, the net effect of a tax, regardless of whom it is imposed upon, is a lower quantity transacted, a higher price paid by the buyer, and a lower amount of revenue received by the seller.

And the same goes for subsidies: The net effect is the same whether the subsidy is given to the buyer or the seller.

What determines how much of a tax the buyer or seller pays (relative to the equilibrium) or how much of a subsidy each receives (relative to the equilibrium) are the supply and demand elasticities. In Figures 6.1 and 6.2, the buyer and seller share the tax and subsidy about equally. That is, in Figure 6.1, P_D is about as far above P_E as P_S is below it. And in Figure 6.2, P_S is about as far above P_E as P_D is below it. But if the elasticities were different, this would not be the case.

Figure 6.3 illustrates the case of a tax when the demand elasticity is low and the supply elasticity is high. In this case, the buyer pays the vast majority of the tax (P_D-P_E) and the seller pays very little (P_E-P_S). It's the entity with the lower elasticity that pays more of a tax, or benefits more from a subsidy.

Figure 6.3: A Tax when Demand Elasticity Is Low, Supply Elasticity High

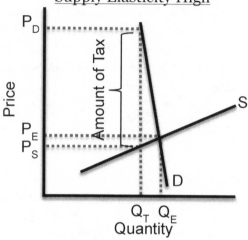

As discussed earlier in this chapter, taxes, by raising the buyer's price and reducing the seller's revenue, decrease quantity transacted relative to the no-tax equilibrium. This means some people don't buy and some sellers aren't able to sell who otherwise would want to. Similarly, subsidies reduce prices and raise revenue, incentivizing transactions that buyers wouldn't otherwise value at the price sellers would have otherwise required at the non-subsidy equilibrium.

These tax-induced or subsidy-induced deviations from equilibrium are examples of "market distortions." Such distortions are some-times worthwhile because some goods create problems or provide benefits not reflected in the market price. Exactly when taxes and subsidies are appropriate and at what level is often controversial, even among economists.

A classic purpose for which taxes are often considered is to reduce or offset pollution. For example, a paper products company might dispose of waste into a nearby river, forcing downstream communities to pay more for water purification. Costs like this pollution are referred to as "negative externalities" because they are borne by parties external to the buy/sell transaction (i.e., by the community at large) rather than by the producer or consumer of the good in question. This negative externality can be addressed by taxing paper products, thereby reducing the quantity used and the corresponding amount of pollution. The tax proceeds could then be used to help downstream communities pay for water treatment.

Other goods such as education provide value beyond that enjoyed by the people receiving the education—a "positive externality." Subsidizing education reduces its cost to students and their families, making it more available than it might be at equilibrium.

Chapter 6 Simple Summary

- A shortage occurs when a price ceiling is imposed below the equilibrium price for a good.

- A surplus occurs when a price floor is imposed above the equilibrium price for a good.

- A tax increases the price paid by consumers, reduces revenue received by suppliers, and reduces the quantity transacted.

- A subsidy reduces the price paid by consumers, increases the revenue received by suppliers, and increases the quantity transacted.

- The party (buyer or seller) with the lower elasticity pays more of a tax and receives more of a subsidy.

- Though government interventions distort the market, they are sometimes justified and supported by society.

PART TWO:

Firm Behavior in Different Types of Markets

CHAPTER SEVEN

Costs of Production

In Part Two of this book, we'll look at the
decisions firms make under different market
conditions. For example, how do the decisions
made by a lone firm serving a market (a "monopoly") differ from the decisions made by firms in
more competitive markets?

As we saw in Chapter 4 when we discussed
supply, a firm's costs of production for a given
good play a role in determining how much the firm
chooses to produce. With a greater understanding
of a firm's costs, we can better understand (and
predict) the decisions the firm makes.

Marginal Cost of Production

As mentioned in Chapter 4, a firm's marginal cost
of production is the additional cost it must incur to

produce one more unit of output. A firm can face decreasing, constant, or increasing marginal costs of production, depending on its level of output, the expense of acquiring additional inputs, and the extent to which they can be used productively.

EXAMPLE: Pauline's Pies is hiring additional employees to increase the number of pizzas the business makes per month. (In what follows, assume all employees are of equivalent skill.)

As shown in the following table, the first employee can produce 250 pizzas per month. Adding a second employee makes the first more productive: Together the first two employees can produce 600 pizzas per month—more than twice what the first employee could do alone. This might be possible if, for example, there are two tasks (e.g., preparing pizzas and tending to ovens) that can be done in parallel with two employees but that must be done sequentially by only one employee. When marginal output increases as more units of input are used, it is known as "increasing marginal returns" (in this case, increasing marginal returns from labor). It's also known as "increasing returns to scale" (*scale* meaning size of the business).

The third employee increases production as much as the second did. Such leveling off of marginal output is known as "constant marginal returns" or "constant returns to scale."

Starting with the fourth employee, each additional employee adds less additional production than the employee before—because there is insufficient space and equipment in the kitchen to keep these new employees fully busy. In fact, once there are five people working at a given time, the kitchen is so full that additional workers would actually *reduce* total production because they would just be getting in the way. In the language of economics, Pauline's Pies faces "diminishing marginal returns from labor" or "decreasing returns to scale" after the third employee. That is, each additional unit of input (labor) brings less output (pizzas) than the previous unit.

Number of Employees	Total Output (pizzas/month)	Marginal Output (pizzas/month)
1	250	250
2	600	350
3	950	350
4	1,200	250
5	1,300	100
6	1,250	-50

Because Pauline's Pies faces diminishing returns from labor after hiring the third worker, it also faces increasing marginal costs of production. For example, as seen in the table above, hiring a fourth employee resulted in 250 additional pizzas being produced per month, whereas hiring a fifth employee only resulted in 100 additional pizzas being produced per month. Assuming that the employees are paid the same hourly wage, the 100 pizzas produced by adding the fifth employee are more costly (per pizza) than the 250 pizzas created by adding the fourth employee.

Fixed vs. Variable Costs

Costs that do not vary as a function of output levels are fixed costs. For Pauline's Pies, fixed costs would include rent, insurance, licenses, and other things the business needs to purchase regardless of how many pizzas it produces. The dollar amount of these costs would be the same regardless of whether the business produces 1,000 or 1,400 pizzas per month. Fixed costs are illustrated with a horizontal line in Figure 7.1.

Variable costs do vary as a function of output (i.e., they go up and down based on how much the firm is producing). For Pauline's Pies, variable costs would include ingredients, employee labor, electricity to run ovens, etc. Variable costs are illustrated with an upward sloping line in Figure 7.1, though in general variable costs may not always grow at the same rate for all levels of output. All costs are either fixed or variable costs. In other words, total costs are equal to fixed costs plus variable costs, as shown in Figure 7.1.

Figure 7.1: Fixed, Variable, and Total Costs

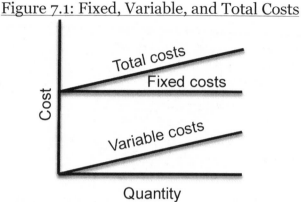

Short Run vs. Long Run

Given enough time, fixed costs can become variable costs. For example, if Pauline's Pies signs one-year leases, rent would be a variable cost over periods longer than one year. That is, over a period of greater than one year, Pauline *would* have the ability to vary the amount she spends on rent by renting a larger or smaller space as necessary to adjust the business's output level.

In economics, the "short run" is the length of time over which a firm's fixed costs are just that—fixed. The "long run" is any length of time longer than the short run. Said differently, in the short run, some costs are variable, while others are fixed. In the long run, all costs are variable.

Sunk Costs Are Irrelevant

In economics, a "sunk cost" is a cost that has been incurred and cannot be recovered, regardless of decisions you make. Sunk costs can (and should) be ignored for decision-making purposes.

EXAMPLE: Pauline's business is growing, and she is looking for a larger kitchen in which to operate. She finds one location that appears suitable, and she pays a non-refundable $400 application fee to rent the place. The next day, she finds another location, for the same amount of monthly rent, with a layout that will permit even more efficient and profitable frozen pizza production.

The application fee that Pauline paid for the first location is a sunk cost. Regardless of which location she decides to rent, she cannot recover the $400. As a result, when choosing whether to rent the first location or the second location, she should ignore the fact that she has spent $400 on an application fee to rent at the first location.

Accounting Costs vs. Economic Costs

A firm's "accounting costs" are all the financial costs it incurs to produce output. For example, for Pauline's Pies, accounting costs would include rent, labor, ingredients, utility bills, insurance, and any licensing fees the business must pay. A firm's "accounting profit" (or loss) is equal to the firm's revenue, minus the firm's accounting costs.

A firm's "economic costs" include the firm's accounting costs as well as opportunity costs. For Pauline's Pies, the economic cost of producing frozen pizzas would include all of the accounting costs listed above, as well as the opportunity cost of producing frozen pizzas (e.g., the profit that the firm could have earned by producing frozen ravioli instead of frozen pizza, if ravioli is the next-most-profitable use of the firm's resources). A firm's "economic profit" (or loss) is equal to the firm's revenue, minus the firm's economic costs.

The concept of economic profit is crucial because firms make decisions based on economic profits rather than accounting profits. That is, firms want to maximize their economic profits rather than accounting profits. Since our focus is economics and not accounting, we use the term "costs" to mean "economic costs" and "profit" to mean "economic profit" unless otherwise indicated.

EXAMPLE: Pauline knows that by running her frozen pizza business, she can bring in $100,000 of revenue per year, with $60,000 of accounting costs. In other words, by running her frozen pizza business, Pauline can earn an accounting profit of $40,000 per year.

Given these facts, does it make sense for Pauline to run her pizza business? We have no way of knowing the answer unless we also know how much Pauline could earn by doing something else.

If Pauline could earn $50,000 per year in accounting profit making frozen raviolis, she would be losing (forgoing) $10,000 per year by making frozen pizza. In other words, the fact that Pauline could generate an *accounting* profit of $40,000 is not a sufficient reason for her to run a frozen pizza business. Pauline is concerned with maximizing her *economic* profit, and due to the $50,000 opportunity cost of making frozen raviolis, her pizza business would actually incur an economic *loss* of $10,000. (That is, overall, Pauline is $10,000 worse-off by running the pizza business than she is if she runs a ravioli business.)

Average Total Costs

A firm's "average total cost" is simply its total costs, divided by the number of units produced. Average total cost is an important concept because a firm cannot earn an economic profit selling a good unless its unit price is above average total cost. For example, if Pauline's Pies incurs costs of $6,000 in a given month and produces 1,000 frozen pizzas that month, the firm's average total cost is $6. If the price of a frozen pizza is above $6, the firm will earn a profit. Otherwise, it will not.

When we plot average total cost on a graph (see Figure 7.2), we see that it takes a U-shape in the presence of increasing marginal costs of production. Average total cost (ATC) is high at low levels of output because the entirety of fixed costs is spread (averaged) over very few units. Then, average total cost falls as output increases, because each additional unit of output costs less than the average (because MC < ATC), thereby bringing the average down. Eventually, however, as marginal costs increase, they grow to exceed average total cost, meaning that each additional unit of output brings the average up. A consequence of this relationship between average total costs and marginal costs is that MC intersects ATC at ATC's minimum.

Figure 7.2: Average Total and Marginal Costs

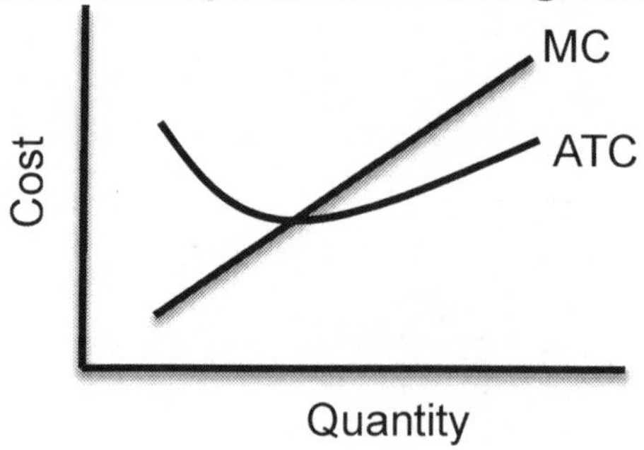

Chapter 7 Simple Summary

- Marginal cost of production is the cost of producing one additional unit of output.

- Most firms face diminishing marginal returns (and, therefore, increasing marginal costs) after some level of output.

- Fixed costs do not vary with production levels. Variable costs do.

- The short run is the time over which fixed costs are fixed. The long run is any length of time greater than the short run.

- Because sunk costs have already been incurred and cannot be recovered, they should be ignored when making decisions.

- Accounting costs include all financial costs. Accounting profit/loss is equal to revenue minus accounting costs.

- Economic costs include accounting plus opportunity costs. Economic profit/loss is equal to revenue minus economic costs. Businesses are concerned with maximizing economic, not accounting, profit.

CHAPTER EIGHT

Perfect Competition

A market is said to be "perfectly competitive" if it meets several requirements, including:

- There are many firms in the market, each of which produces an identical product, and each of which represents only a very small portion of the total market.
- There are no "barriers to entry," meaning that firms are free to enter (or leave) the market as they please.
- Buyers and sellers each have "perfect information," meaning, for example, that each buyer knows exactly how much utility he/she would derive from purchasing the good and each seller knows the most efficient way to produce the good.
- There are no externalities. That is, the benefit of the good in question goes entirely to

the buyers of the good, and the costs of production are borne entirely by the producers.
- Each firm in the market is chiefly concerned with maximizing profit.

No market is *perfectly* competitive, but some get closer to the ideal than others. Agricultural commodities (e.g., oranges) are the classic example of a nearly-perfectly-competitive market.

Firms Are Price Takers

In a perfectly competitive market, firms are "price takers." That is, they have no ability to influence the market price for the good they produce.

EXAMPLE: Oliver is an orange farmer. The oranges he grows are not noticeably different from the oranges grown by countless other farmers around the world. As a result, Oliver has no ability to charge a premium price. If he charges anything more than the market price for oranges, he won't be able to sell any oranges at all.

On the other hand, because Oliver's farm produces just a very tiny portion of the world's total orange production, Oliver will have no trouble selling all of his oranges at the market price.

In other words, Oliver cannot charge more than the market price, and he has no reason to charge less. Oliver is a price taker.

Making Decisions at the Margin

The term "marginal revenue" refers to how much additional revenue a firm would earn from one additional unit of output. As a rule, any time the marginal revenue for the next unit of output exceeds the marginal cost of production, a profit-maximizing firm will make that unit of output.

EXAMPLE: Figure 8.1 shows the marginal revenue (MR) and marginal cost (MC) curves for Oliver's orange farm.

Figure 8.1: MR and MC in Perfect Competition

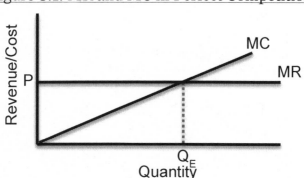

Because Oliver is operating in a perfectly competitive market, and because he is therefore a price taker, Oliver's marginal revenue curve is a flat line at the market price (P) for a bushel of oranges. That is, no matter how much Oliver is currently producing, one additional bushel of oranges will bring in an amount of revenue equal to the market price for a bushel of oranges.

Oliver's marginal cost curve is upward sloping because Oliver faces increasing marginal costs of production.

Given the marginal cost and marginal revenue curves shown in the figure, Oliver will choose to produce at quantity Q_E because that is his profit-maximizing quantity. That is, if he is currently producing at a quantity less than Q_E, he could produce more units and increase his profit because the marginal revenue for those units would be greater than the marginal cost of production for those units. But once he reaches output level Q_E, he will not produce additional units because his marginal cost for creating those units would be greater than the marginal revenue he would receive from those units.

Even though Oliver maximizes his profit by producing at quantity Q_E, it may not be the case that his profit is actually positive. That is, he could be losing money, albeit the least amount possible (because he has maximized profit).

Calculating Profit or Loss

When we add an average total cost curve to the previous figure, we can determine whether Oliver is earning a profit or incurring a loss.

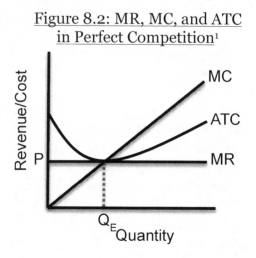

Figure 8.2: MR, MC, and ATC
in Perfect Competition[1]

We already know that Oliver will choose to produce at the quantity (Q_E) at which marginal cost

---

[1] Some readers may begin to feel uneasy about charts with more than two curves, as Figure 8.2 and later ones have. One way to demystify such charts is to first recognize the curves you've seen before (MC and MR in Figure 8.2, for example). Then, identify each new curve (just ATC in Figure 8.2) and understand what it adds to the story (as explained in the text).

equals marginal revenue. So what we want to know is how Oliver's total (not marginal) costs compare to his total (not marginal) revenue at quantity Q_E.

At any given point of production, Oliver's total revenue (TR) is equal to the market price per bushel of oranges (P), multiplied by the quantity of bushels he produces (Q). That is:

$$TR = P \times Q.$$

And at any given level of production, Oliver's total costs (TC) are equal to the average total cost of production (ATC) at that point, multiplied by the quantity produced (Q). That is:

$$TC = ATC \times Q. \text{ (Remember, ATC is TC} \div \text{Q.)}$$

So when producing at quantity Q_E, Oliver's profit (or loss, if negative) will be calculated as:

$$\text{Profit} = (P \times Q_E) - (ATC \times Q_E), \text{ or}$$

$$\text{Profit} = (P - ATC) \times Q_E.$$

If the market price (P) is greater than Oliver's average total cost (ATC) at quantity Q_E, Oliver will earn a positive profit (i.e., the expression above will be positive). If Oliver's average total cost at quantity Q_E exceeds the market price, Oliver will incur a negative profit (i.e., a loss, because the expression will be negative). As it turns out, in Figure 8.2, Oliver is earning neither a profit nor a loss because ATC and P are equal at Q_E. As explained next, this is always the case in the long run in a perfectly competitive market.

Zero Profits in the Long Run

As discussed previously, in a perfectly competitive market, there are no barriers to entry or exit; firms are able to enter or leave the market as they please.

As a result, if profit-maximizing firms in a perfectly competitive market were earning profits, other firms would enter the market to grab a share of the profits. When new firms enter the market, supply increases, causing the price of the good to fall (as discussed in Chapter 5), thereby resulting in smaller profits for firms already in the market. In fact, this phenomenon (firms entering the market, causing a decline in price) will continue until the price has fallen to a level at which firms are earning exactly zero profit, thereby leaving no incentive for additional firms to enter the market. (A similar argument can be made about firms exiting the market if they are incurring a loss.)

We know from earlier in this chapter that a firm in perfect competition earns exactly zero profit when the market price for the good it sells is equal to the firm's average total cost for producing that good (i.e., P = ATC). We also know that profit-maximizing firms choose to produce at the point at which marginal revenue—defined as the market price—is equal to marginal cost of production (i.e., P = MC). In other words, in the long run, in a perfectly competitive market, each firm produces at the point at which marginal cost, average total cost, and price are all equal. Figure 8.2 (earlier) shows such a situation. Also, Figure 8.2 applies to every firm in the market because one of the assumptions of perfect competition is that all firms have the knowledge and ability to produce most efficiently. That is, they all have the same marginal and average cost curves.

The fact that firms earn zero profits in the long run in a perfectly competitive market is generally considered to be good for society. It means, among other things, that consumers are paying the lowest prices necessary to get firms to produce what they're producing. (Remember, while these firms have no economic profits, they still have accounting profits.)

Firms Producing at Their Lowest Average Cost

An additional societal benefit of perfect competition is that, in the long run, firms are forced to produce at the lowest cost possible. You can see

71

this by looking again at Figure 8.2 and confirming that at Q$_E$, the firm's ATC curve is at its lowest point (i.e., the point at which it intersects the marginal cost of production curve).

Producing at a Loss in the Short Run

In the short run, a firm may continue to operate even if it is incurring a loss. The explanation for this sort of behavior lies in the difference between fixed and variable costs.

EXAMPLE: Oliver has fixed costs of $20,000 per month. When he produces at his ideal level of production (where MC = MR, as discussed earlier), he earns $40,000 of revenue and incurs $25,000 of variable costs. At this level of production, Oliver has a total loss of $5,000 ($40,000 revenue, minus $45,000 total costs).

If Oliver completely stopped production, however, he would have a loss of $20,000 due to his fixed costs. In other words, given these facts, Oliver cannot earn a profit. But by producing at MC = MR, he can at least minimize his loss (because he has maximized his profit, even though it's negative).

Once Oliver's fixed costs expire, however, he will probably be best served by choosing not to renew them (i.e., shutting down his business completely), unless he expects circumstances to change (e.g., an increase in the price of his product that would allow him to operate profitably).

Consumer and Producer Surplus

"Consumer surplus" refers to the value that consumers derive from purchasing a good. For example, if you would be willing to spend $10 on a good, but you are able to purchase it for just $7, your consumer surplus from the transaction is $3. You're getting $3 more value from the good than it cost you.

We can use a chart of supply and demand to show consumer surplus in a market.

EXAMPLE: Figure 8.3 shows the perfectly competitive market for oranges. The market is in equilibrium at P_E and Q_E. As we know, the demand curve indicates consumers' *willingness* to pay. In Figure 8.3, the amount that consumers actually *are* paying is P_E—the equilibrium market price for oranges. For each transaction that occurs up to Q_E, consumer surplus is achieved in an amount equal to the distance between the demand curve and P_E. As a result, the shaded area in Figure 8.3 indicates the total consumer surplus achieved in the orange market.

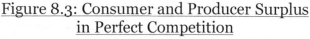

Figure 8.3: Consumer and Producer Surplus
in Perfect Competition

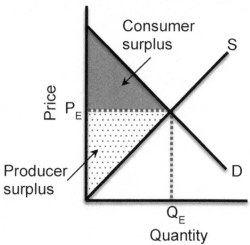

"Producer surplus" refers to the value that *producers* derive from transactions. For example, if a producer would be willing to sell a good for $4, but he is able to sell it for $10, he achieves producer surplus of $6.

Like consumer surplus, producer surplus can also be shown via a chart of supply and demand. This time, however, the surplus from each transaction is represented by the distance between the *supply* curve (which denotes the lowest price suppliers would be willing to accept) and the market price. The total producer surplus achieved in the orange market would be represented by the dotted area in Figure 8.3.

"Total surplus" refers to the sum of consumer surplus and producer surplus. Total surplus is maximized in perfect competition because free-market equilibrium is reached. That is, if a quantity less than the free-market equilibrium quantity were transacted, total surplus would be less, because there would be beneficial transactions that are failing to occur (i.e., transactions where consumers' willingness to pay is greater than the lowest price suppliers are willing to accept). And if a quantity *greater* than the free-market equilibrium quantity were transacted, total surplus would be less, because transactions that cost more to producers than consumers would be willing to pay would occur.[1]

---

[1] The government-related topics discussed in Chapter 6 can also be assessed from a total surplus standpoint. That is, in an otherwise-perfectly-competitive market, taxes, subsidies, price ceilings below the free-market equilibrium price, and price floors above the free-market equilibrium price all result in reduced total surplus. Yet, such actions are still taken when society decides that the benefits outweigh the costs. Alternatively, such actions are sometimes advantageous from a purely economic standpoint. They can sometimes *increase* total surplus when the market is not perfectly competitive, if government intervention can bring the market closer to that ideal.

Chapter 8 Simple Summary

- In a perfectly competitive market, there are many firms making identical products.

- In a perfectly competitive market, firms cannot influence the market price. As a result, each firm's marginal revenue curve is equal to the market price (P = MR).

- In a perfectly competitive market, each firm has the same marginal cost curve, because each firm knows how to produce with maximum efficiency.

- To maximize profit (or minimize loss), firms will produce at the point at which their marginal revenue equals their marginal cost of production (where MR = MC).

- In perfect competition, firms will enter or leave the market until the market price is such that each firm earns exactly zero economic profit and produces at its lowest possible cost. (Remember, zero economic profit does not mean zero accounting profit.)

- Total surplus is maximized in a perfectly competitive market.

CHAPTER NINE

Monopoly

When there is only one supplier in a market, that supplier is known as a "monopoly." In a monopoly market, there are barriers to entry that prevent new firms from entering the market. Because of these barriers to entry, monopolies have no competition and can make different decisions than firms in a perfectly competitive market. In addition, monopoly markets can have different outcomes than competitive markets.

Monopolies Have Market Power

Because it has no competition, a monopoly is *not* a price taker. That is, unlike firms in a perfectly competitive market, a monopoly can raise the price of the good it sells without immediately losing all of its sales. When a firm has the ability to profitably raise the price of its product above the price that would occur in a perfectly competitive market, the firm is said to have "market power."

EXAMPLE: Marty owns a small-scale ski park in a location far from any other site suitable for skiing (so, in Marty's local market, his business is a monopoly). Because Marty has no competition, he can charge whatever price he wants for admission to his park, and he can test different prices to see which is the most profitable.

Marginal Revenue for a Monopoly

Assuming that a monopoly must charge each customer the same price for its good, the monopoly faces a downward sloping marginal revenue curve—meaning that each additional unit the firm sells brings in less revenue than the unit before. The reason for this declining marginal revenue is that the firm must reduce the price it charges for its product if it wants to sell more units. And that new lower price would apply to *all* units sold— including all the units sold to buyers who would have been willing to pay a higher price.

EXAMPLE: Figure 9.1 shows the demand curve and the resulting marginal revenue curve for Marty's ski park monopoly.

Figure 9.1 Demand and Marginal Revenue Curves for Marty's Ski Park (Monopoly)[1]

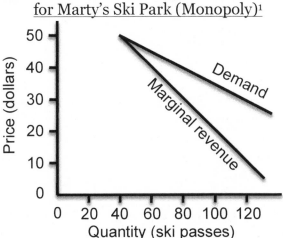

If he charges $50 for a day pass, Marty can sell 40 passes per day—for a total daily revenue of $2,000. Marty's marginal revenue for the first 40 passes is $50 per pass.

If Marty reduces the price to $40, he can sell 80 passes per day—for a total daily revenue of $3,200. The marginal revenue for the 40 additional passes sold is $1,200 (i.e., $3,200 minus $2,000), or $30 per pass.

If Marty reduces the price further to $30, he can sell 120 passes each day—for a total daily

---

[1] For a monopoly, if the demand curve is a straight line, the marginal revenue curve will also be a straight line, with exactly twice the slope of the demand curve.

revenue of $3,600. The marginal revenue for the additional 40 passes sold is $400 (i.e., $3,600 minus $3,200), or just $10 per pass.

Marty faces declining marginal revenue (i.e., each additional pass sold brings in less additional revenue than the previous pass) because when he reduces his price to sell more passes, he reduces the price that *every* visitor to the park pays—even those visitors who would have paid a higher price.

Maximizing Profit by Producing at MC = MR

Just like firms in perfect competition, monopolies choose to produce each unit for which marginal revenue exceeds marginal cost. That is, they produce up to the point at which marginal revenue is equal to marginal cost because this is the point at which the firm's profit is maximized. (See "Making Decisions at the Margin" in Chapter 8.)

Profits and Losses for Monopolies

As with firms in competition, a monopoly doesn't necessarily earn a profit just because it is producing at its profit-maximizing level of output. It could still be incurring a loss—just the smallest loss possible. Whether a monopoly earns profit or loss depends on how the firm's average total cost of production at its profit-maximizing output compares to the price at that level of output. (This is no different than with a firm in competition—see "Calculating Profit or Loss" in Chapter 8.)

EXAMPLE: Phoenix Pharmaceutical is a monopoly because it has a patent for its good (a drug). We can see in Figure 9.2 that this monopoly is earning a profit because the monopoly price, P_M (i.e., the point on the demand curve, D, corresponding to quantity Q_M) is greater than ATC at Q_M.

Figure 9.2 A Profit-Earning Monopoly

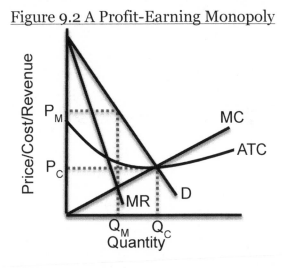

What *is* different about a monopoly (relative to a firm in perfect competition) is that it can earn a profit in the long run as well as the short run. In perfect competition, firms' profits eventually disappear as new firms enter the market and drive the price downward to the competitive price (P_C in Figure 9.2). In the case of a monopoly, barriers to entry (like the patent owned by our hypothetical pharmaceutical company) prevent new firms from entering the market. That's why it's a *monopoly*.

Monopolies: Producing at a Higher Average Cost

A significant negative trait of monopolies is that their profit-maximizing level of output is *not* the point at which they are producing at the lowest possible cost per unit, as would be the case in a perfectly competitive market. As a result, when left to operate as they please, monopolies produce at a higher average cost of production than is necessary. You can see this in Figure 9.2. At Q_M, ATC is *not* at its lowest point, but at Q_C—the quantity that would be produced under perfect competition—the ATC curve *is* at its lowest point.

Loss of Surplus with a Monopoly

Because monopolies have a declining marginal revenue curve, they naturally produce less output than would be produced in a competitive market. That is, they restrict their output in order to maximize profit (keeping the price of their product higher than the competitive price).

EXAMPLE: In Figure 9.3, Q_M (the quantity at which MC = MR) is the profit-maximizing quantity of output for Phoenix Pharmaceutical, the monopoly introduced in the previous example. Q_C is what the firm's profit-maximizing quantity of output *would* be if it were operating in a perfectly competitive marketplace (and it therefore faced a horizontal MR curve at P_C). Notice that $Q_M < Q_C$.

Figure 9.3 Monopoly Deadweight Loss.

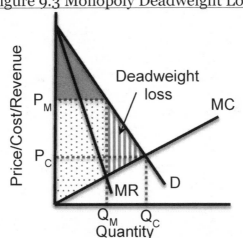

A consequence of a monopoly's profit-maximizing decision to restrict output is a reduction in total surplus relative to that of a perfectly competitive market. The amount by which surplus is reduced is known as a "deadweight loss." Figure 9.3 illustrates consumer surplus in a monopoly market (the solid, shaded region between the monopoly price, P_M, and the demand curve, D); the producer surplus (the dotted region between marginal cost, MC, and the monopoly price, P_M); and the deadweight loss (the horizontally striped region). This horizontally striped region represents the deadweight loss of this monopoly market relative to a perfectly competitive one; it is the additional surplus that would have occurred if the market were perfectly competitive (i.e., if transactions had occurred all the way up to Q_C rather than just Q_M).

Monopolies and Government

Because monopolies generally have a detrimental economic effect (i.e., a reduction in total surplus), governments sometimes choose to end a monopoly by forcing the firm to break up into smaller firms (which will then presumably compete with each other). The laws that allow a government to break up (or otherwise regulate) a monopoly are known as "antitrust laws."

In some cases, however, governments allow a monopoly to exist because the benefits outweigh the drawbacks. For example, utility businesses (e.g., electric companies, gas companies) require enormous amounts of infrastructure. And it would not be cost-effective to build duplicate sets of infrastructure just for the sake of competition. Industries like this—in which one producer can supply the good in question at a lower average cost than multiple producers—are known as "natural monopolies." While governments often allow such natural monopolies to exist, they frequently choose to regulate them so that output and price are closer to competitive levels. Such regulations might include subsidizing production costs, regulating the price of the good in question, or simply imposing a requirement that the monopoly produce at least a certain amount of output. In some cases, governments will require the monopoly to allow potential competitors to use its infrastructure for a reasonable fee.

In other cases, governments even choose to *create* a monopoly. For example, when a patent is granted to an inventor, that inventor is given a monopoly over the market for the invention (until the patent expires). Governments choose to do this as a way to spur innovation, by making it more appealing (i.e., profitable) to invent things. Perhaps it goes without saying, but when and how to allow, break up, or regulate monopolies is often debated, even among economists.

Chapter 9 Simple Summary

- A monopoly is a firm with no competition.

- A monopoly has market power. That is, it can profitably increase the price of the good it sells by reducing the output it produces.

- Monopolies face downward sloping marginal revenue curves.

- Like other firms, monopolies maximize profit (or minimize loss) by producing at the point where marginal revenue equals marginal cost of production.

- To maximize profit, monopolies restrict their production below what would be produced in a competitive market. The resulting lower output and higher price cause a deadweight loss to society.

- To address the deadweight loss, in some cases, governments will enforce antitrust laws to break up or otherwise regulate a monopoly.

CHAPTER TEN

Oligopoly

An "oligopoly" is an industry dominated by a few firms (as few as two), with barriers to entry that make it difficult for new firms to enter the industry. The automotive industry (dominated by companies such as Toyota, General Motors, Ford, and Honda) is a current example of an oligopoly.

Firms Are Not Price Takers

In an oligopoly, because there are only a few sellers, each seller's actions *do* have an impact on market price. For example, if Honda were to flood the market with Civics, the price of small sedans (both Civics and those from other automakers) would fall. Because firms in an oligopoly can influence the price of their product by changing output levels, they face downward sloping marginal revenue curves—much like a monopoly faces.

Collusion in an Oligopoly

In some cases, firms in an oligopoly will compete very aggressively, thereby resulting in an outcome that is close to that of a perfectly competitive market (i.e., a higher level of output and lower price than would occur with a monopoly and no or low profits for firms in the market).

In other cases, the firms in an oligopoly will recognize that by competing as hard as possible, they drive the market price (and their profits) downward. As a result, instead of competing, the firms choose to "collude" (i.e., cooperate) by agreeing to cut back on production to keep the market price (and their profits) up. This type of behavior is known as acting as a "cartel." Essentially, cartel behavior takes a competitive market and turns it into a monopoly, with each firm getting a share of the monopoly's profits.

When everything goes as planned, cartel behavior is the profit-maximizing strategy for the industry. And, in turn, because it is a monopoly-like outcome, cartel behavior is bad for society in that it results in a deadweight loss (i.e., forgone surplus, due to a higher price and less output than would occur in a more competitive market).

OPEC (Organization of the Petroleum Exporting Countries) is an example of a modern cartel. It consists of several oil-producing countries (e.g., Saudi Arabia, Iran, Iraq) that attempt to coordinate their policies in order to secure profits.

Cheating the Cartel

The problem with collusion (from the perspective of the cartel) is that each firm has an incentive to cheat by producing more than the agreed upon amount. If only one firm cheats, the cheating firm, by selling additional units at a profitable price, will earn a greater profit than if it cooperated.

In some cases, cartels break down because every firm cheats—with the end result being the competitive outcome discussed earlier (i.e., higher level of output, lower prices, and lower profits).[1]

Government Intervention

In many countries, including the United States, antitrust laws typically prohibit firms from explicitly colluding for the sake of reducing competition.

---

[1] This discussion of cartel behavior is a small piece of the microeconomic subdiscipline of game theory—the analysis of strategies in competitive environments.

When firms in an oligopoly appear to be colluding, governments will sometimes break up or otherwise regulate the largest firm(s).

Chapter 10 Simple Summary

- An oligopoly is an industry dominated by just a few firms.

- Because each firm in an oligopoly makes up a significant part of the market, firms' behavior has an effect on the market price of the good in question.

- An oligopoly market can be highly competitive, or it can have the properties of a monopoly, depending on how firms behave.

- In an oligopoly, firms sometimes collude (act as a cartel) in order to secure profits by reducing output and driving up the market price of the good in question.

- Cartels often fail due to the incentive that each firm has to cheat.

- In many countries, cartel behavior is prohibited via antitrust laws.

CHAPTER ELEVEN

Monopolistic Competition

A "monopolistically competitive" market is one in which there are many sellers competing not only on price but also on the basis of small differences in their products, known as "product differentiation." In other words, their products are similar enough to be in competition with one another, but they are not perfect substitutes.

The market for wine is an example of monopolistic competition. Because each producer (i.e., vineyard) makes a product that is somewhat different than the product of other producers, each can achieve sales without having to match the price of their lowest-price competitor. That is, each seller has some degree of market power (though less market power than firms in less competitive circumstances such as monopolies).

Making Decisions at the Margin

As with firms in other market circumstances, firms in monopolistic competition choose to produce at the point where marginal revenue equals marginal cost because that is the point at which they maximize their profit (or minimize their loss).

And, like monopolies and firms in an oligopoly, firms in monopolistic competition face downward sloping marginal revenue curves because their decisions to increase or decrease output will have an impact on the market price of their product. (As a reminder, this is in contrast to firms in perfect competition, which cannot influence the market price of their product and which therefore face a horizontal marginal revenue curve, as discussed in Chapter 8.)

No Profits in the Long Run

Monopolistically competitive markets have no (or low) barriers to entry. As a result, as with a perfectly competitive market, firms should have no profits or losses in the long run. Remember, this is the result of new firms *entering* the market in the presence of short run profits, thereby driving prices downward (until profits are zero), and the result of firms *leaving* the market in the presence of short run losses, thereby driving prices upward (until losses are zero).

EXAMPLE: Violet's Vineyard operates in a monopolistically competitive market. Figure 11.1 depicts the long run (i.e., zero-profit) outcome faced by this firm. We know the firm is earning exactly zero profit because ATC = P at the firm's profit-maximizing quantity (i.e., where MR = MC).

Figure 11.1: Monopolistic Competition
Long Run Equilibrium

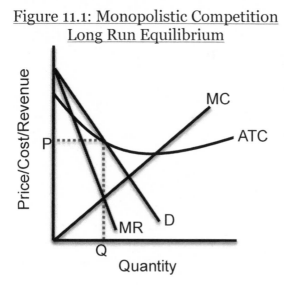

Firms Do Not Produce at Lowest Cost

From a societal perspective, one negative outcome of monopolistic competition is that, like a monopoly, firms in monopolistic competition do not produce at the lowest-cost level of output. That is, as a result of their downward sloping marginal revenue curves (and their resulting incentive to restrict production to maximize profits), they produce at a lower level of output than the level at which average total cost is minimized. This can be seen in Figure 11.1. ATC is not at its lowest point at the profit-maximizing level of output (Q).

Loss of Surplus with Monopolistic Competition

Monopolistic competition also results in a deadweight loss to society (relative to perfect competition) because of the higher market price and lower quantity transacted that result from firms' incentive to restrict output to increase profits. (This is much the same as the monopoly outcome illustrated in Figure 9.3.)

On the other hand, monopolistic competition does have a positive outcome in the sense that consumers have a variety of differentiated products from which to choose.

Chapter 11 Simple Summary

- A monopolistically competitive market is one in which there are many sellers competing on price as well as on the basis of product differentiation.

- Firms in monopolistic competition have some degree of market power because their products are differentiated from the products of their competitors.

- Because firms in monopolistic competition have market power (i.e., the market price of their product is impacted by their decisions of how much to produce), they face downward sloping marginal revenue curves.

- Due to no (or low) barriers to entry, firms in a monopolistically competitive market earn no economic profit in the long run. (Remember, a firm with exactly zero economic profit *is* earning an accounting profit.)

- Like monopolies and oligopolies, monopolistically competitive markets are productively inefficient because firms in such markets do not produce at the lowest-cost level of output.

CONCLUSION

The Insights and Limitations of Economics

Economics seeks to explain why entities make the decisions that they do. However, given the complexity of the real world, economics can only provide us with imperfect models of decision-making. Still, even imperfect models can be useful.

For example, many basic models in economics assume that every individual's goal is to maximize his or her utility (happiness). To maximize your utility, you must spend each dollar of your budget on the good that offers you the highest marginal utility for that dollar. Of course, in the real world, people do not do any sort of quantitative marginal utility calculations when choosing how to spend their money. But the overall concept still holds: People spend their money in whatever way they think will make them most happy—which usually means buying a variety of goods and services due to the fact that most goods provide decreasing marginal utility (i.e., each additional unit consumed brings less additional happiness than the prior unit).

Economics shows us that specialization and trade make everybody better off. In a world with few constraints on trade, we're better off with doctors, farmers, and homebuilders than we would be if everybody tried to handle their own medical needs, grow their own food, and make their own home. However, though this may be true in general and in the long run, sometimes free trade can impose short-term disruptions. For example, when tariffs are lifted on imports of a good, native producers of that good (and their workers) who were protected by those tariffs may be displaced.

When allowed to trade as they please, buyers and sellers acting in their own best interests will naturally drive a market toward equilibrium—the point at which quantity demanded is equal to quantity supplied. In the real world, however, many markets are affected by various forms of government intervention. While such government interventions can distort the market, they are sometimes justified and supported by society. In addition, even without government intervention, many markets don't conform to the assumptions required to achieve free-market equilibrium. For example, buyers and sellers cannot always process and understand all relevant information, thereby leading to suboptimal out-comes.

Microeconomics is especially concerned with the decisions made by individual firms. As a rule, to maximize economic profit (or minimize economic loss), firms will produce every unit for which marginal revenue is greater than marginal cost. That is, they will produce up to the point at which their marginal revenue is equal to their marginal cost of production. This, of course, presumes firms are profit-maximizing entities. Not all firms are. For example, some hospitals forgo additional profit in order to provide charity care.

The outcome in a given market naturally depends on various characteristics of the market—especially the degree of competition among firms.

In a perfectly competitive market (an ideal which no real-life market ever reaches), firms will enter or leave the market until the market price is such that each firm earns exactly zero economic profits while producing at its lowest possible cost of production—a good thing for society. In addition, total surplus is maximized in a perfectly competitive market because the free-market equilibrium is reached, meaning that everybody who wants to purchase the good at its current price is able to do so, and every producer who wants to sell at the current price is able to do so.

At the opposite end of the spectrum is a monopoly market, in which there is only one firm (i.e., no competition at all). To maximize profit, monopolies restrict their production below what would be produced in a competitive market. The resulting lower output and higher price causes a deadweight loss to society (i.e., a reduction in total surplus). In some cases, to address the deadweight loss, governments will enforce antitrust laws to break up or otherwise regulate a monopoly.

An oligopoly—a market dominated by a few firms—can be highly competitive, or it can have the properties of a monopoly, depending on whether the firms choose to cooperate (i.e., act as a cartel) or compete aggressively. In most cases, however, the outcome will be somewhere between that of a monopoly market and a perfectly competitive market.

In a monopolistically competitive market, there are many firms competing not only on the basis of price, but also on the basis of product differentiation. Firms earn no economic profits in the long run, but as with a monopoly or oligopoly, there is still a deadweight loss because firms produce a lower quantity at a higher price than would be produced in a perfectly competitive market.

Maximizing utility, surplus, and economic profit are the domains of economics, but they are clearly not the only things of value to society. In addition to being concerned with economic efficiency (utility maximization), we are also concerned with *fairness* or equity. For example, while it might be more economically efficient to allow a market for votes (in which people who wish to do so could sell their vote for public office candidates to the highest bidder), most people believe that would not be fair and equitable. Poor people would have a permanent disadvantage in the resulting political environment. Voting markets would also change our view of the relationship between society and government. Instead of a civic duty, voting would be a commodity. For these and other reasons, it strikes most people as culturally wrong or fundamentally unjust to allow votes to be bought and sold, which reflects the fact that we have values beyond that of economic efficiency.

Economics is useful, but incomplete. Economic models are powerful, but approximate. Other areas of economics not considered in this book (like behavioral economics and game theory) broaden the scope of economics and offer additional insights, but they too have limitations. Fundamentally, economics offers important considerations for some problems, but not the *only* important considerations for *every* problem.

APPENDIX A

Helpful Resources

The following list includes resources that can help you learn more about microeconomics and other areas of economics. Most are free or very inexpensive.

Books:

Economics: A Very Short Introduction, by Partha Dasgupta

Economics For Dummies, by Sean Flynn, PhD

Modern Principles: Microeconomics, by Tyler Cowen and Alex Tabarrok

Online Resources:

Marginal Revolution University:
http://mruniversity.com/

EconLib and EconTalk:
http://www.econlib.org/ and
http://www.econtalk.org/

WikiEducator's list of free, online economics texts:
http://tinyurl.com/econtexts

There is also a list of microeconomics e-books, at:
http://tinyurl.com/econ-ebooks

And finally, a list of other economics resources
available at Austin's blog:
http://tinyurl.com/economics-resources

APPENDIX B

Glossary

absolute advantage: a situation in which one producer requires fewer units of input relative to another producer to make the same amount of output

accounting costs: costs for which an actual monetary outlay is made (e.g., rent, supplies, labor, but not opportunity cost, defined later)

accounting profit/loss: calculated as revenue minus accounting costs

allocative efficiency: a situation in which resources are being used to produce the types and quantities of goods most valued by society

antitrust laws: the set of laws that allow governments to break up or otherwise regulate markets with no (or very little) competition

ATC: see average total cost

average total cost: total costs of production, divided by total units produced

barriers to entry: circumstances that prevent new firms from entering a market

cartel: a group of firms in an oligopoly market that have chosen to cooperate by cutting back on production to keep prices (and their profits) up

collusion: the act of cooperating as a cartel

comparative advantage: a situation in which one producer has a lower opportunity cost than another producer in the production of a good

consumer surplus: the benefit that consumers derive from being able to purchase goods at prices lower than the maximum price they would be willing to pay

D: see demand

deadweight loss: the total surplus that is for-gone due to market inefficiencies (e.g., deviation from perfect competition)

demand: the amount of a good that consumers will purchase at various prices

economic costs: the sum of accounting costs and opportunity costs

economic profit/loss: calculated as revenue minus economic costs

elasticity of demand: a measure of price sensitivity exhibited by consumers of a good (i.e., the degree to which quantity demanded changes in response to changes in price); formally, the percentage change in quantity demanded divided by the percentage change in price

elasticity of supply: a measure of the degree of price sensitivity exhibited by suppliers of a good (i.e., the degree to which quantity supplied changes in response to changes in price); formally, the percentage change in quantity supplied divided by the percentage change in price

equilibrium price: the price at which a good's supply and demand curves meet

equilibrium quantity: the quantity at which a good's supply and demand curves meet

factors of production: the scarce (i.e., limited) inputs that society uses to create goods: land, labor, capital, and human capital

fixed costs: costs that do not vary as a function of output

marginal cost of production: the additional cost that must be incurred in order to produce one additional unit of output

marginal revenue: the additional revenue that would be earned from the production of one additional unit of output

marginal utility: the additional utility derived from the consumption of one additional unit of a good

market equilibrium: an outcome in which quantity supplied and quantity demanded are equal; where the supply and demand curves intersect

market power: a firm's ability to profitably raise the price of its product

MC: see marginal cost of production

monopolistic competition: a type of market in which many sellers compete not only on price but also on the basis of product differentiation

monopoly: a market in which there is only one supplier

MR: see marginal revenue

negative externality: a cost incurred in the production of a good that is borne by parties other than the producer and consumer of the good in question

oligopoly: a market dominated by just a few suppliers

opportunity cost: the utility of the best alternative that an economic entity must forgo in order to make a given choice

perfect competition: a type of market that meets several requirements, including: many profit-maximizing suppliers, each of which makes an identical product; no barriers to entry; no positive or negative externalities; and perfect information on behalf of both consumers and producers

positive externality: a benefit resulting from the production of a good that is enjoyed by parties other than the producer and consumer of the good in question

price ceiling: a government-imposed maximum price for a good

price floor: a government-imposed minimum price for a good

price taker: a firm with no ability to influence the market price of the good it produces (i.e., a firm with no market power)

producer surplus: the benefit that producers derive from being able to sell goods at prices higher than the minimum price they would be willing to accept

production possibilities frontier: a chart that conveys the various choices an entity could make when choosing what to produce; the set of choices that are most productively efficient

productive efficiency: a situation in which every good is being produced using the fewest possible resources

quantity demanded: the number of units of a good that are demanded at a given price

quantity supplied: the number of units of a good that are supplied at a given price

S: see supply

shortage: circumstances in which quantity demanded exceeds quantity supplied

sunk cost: a cost that has already been incurred and that cannot be recovered, regardless of decisions you make. Sunk costs should be ignored for decision-making purposes.

supply: the amount of a good that producers will produce at various prices

surplus: circumstances in which quantity supplied exceeds quantity demanded. (Note that "surplus" means something completely different in this context than it means in the context of consumer surplus, producer surplus, or total surplus.)

total cost: the sum of fixed costs and variable costs

total surplus: the sum of consumer surplus and producer surplus

utility: a person or society's overall happiness

variable costs: costs that vary as a function of output

Acknowledgments

We would like to thank Julian Jamison and Wade Pfau for generously contributing their time and subject matter expertise. Special thanks also go to the Simple Subjects editing team—Michelle, Debbi, and Kalinda—for once again working hard to make a complex subject understandable.

About the Authors

Austin Frakt is a health economist with the Department of Veterans Affairs and an associate professor at Boston University. He does research in health policy and economics and has published in the top peer-reviewed journals in his field. He founded and is co-editor in chief of the health policy blog TheIncidentalEconomist.com and is a regular contributor to *The New York Times*.

Mike Piper is the author of several personal finance books as well as the popular blog ObliviousInvestor.com. He is a Missouri licensed CPA. Mike's writing has been featured in many places, including *The Wall Street Journal*, *MarketWatch*, *Forbes*, and *Morningstar*.

Other Books in the *in 100 Pages or Less* Series

INDEX

Made in the USA
Middletown, DE
19 August 2017